UPS AND DOWNS

Senior Authors
Carl B. Smith
Ronald Wardhaugh

Macmillan Publishing Co., Inc.
New York

Collier Macmillan Publishers
London

SERIES **r**

Macmillan Reading

This work is also published together with other works in a
single volume under the title: *Opening Doors,* copyright
© 1980 Macmillan Publishing Co., Inc. Parts of this work
were published in SERIES r: The New Macmillan Reading
Program.

Macmillan Publishing Co., Inc.
866 Third Avenue
New York, New York 10022
Collier Macmillan Canada, Ltd.

Printed in the United States of America
ISBN 0-02-128320-6
98765432

ACKNOWLEDGMENTS

The publisher gratefully acknowledges permission to reprint the following copyrighted material:

"The Donkey Knows," adapted from "I Think I Know," from *Fried Onions and Marshmallows* by Sally Melcher Jarvis. Copyright © 1968 by Sally Melcher Jarvis. By permission of Parents' Magazine Press.

"I Woke Up One Morning," from *A Rumbudgin of Nonsense* by Arnold Spilka. Copyright © 1970 by Arnold Spilka. Reprinted by permission of Arnold Spilka.

"I wonder how it feels to fly . . . ," adapted from *The Turquoise Horse* edited by Flora Hood. Copyright © 1972 by Flora Hood. Reprinted by permission of G.P. Putnam's Sons and Curtis Brown, Ltd.

"If I Were a . . . ," from *The Rose On My Cake* by Karla Kuskin. Copyright © 1964 by Karla Kuskin. By permission of Harper & Row, Publishers, Inc.

"Look," from *All That Sunlight* by Charlotte Zolotow. Copyright © 1967 by Charlotte Zolotow. By permission of Harper & Row, Publishers, Inc.

"Silly Sam," adapted from *Silly Sam* by Leonore Klein. Copyright © 1969 by Scholastic Magazines, Inc. Reprinted by permission of Scholastic Magazines, Inc.

"Things in the Pool," from *Little Raccoon and Poems From The Woods* by Lilian Moore. Copyright © 1975 by Lilian Moore. By permission of McGraw-Hill Book Company.

"Things That Go Together," from *Just Think!* by Betty Miles and Joan Blos. Copyright © 1971 by Betty Miles. Reprinted by permission of Alfred A. Knopf, Inc.

"Tree House," from *Where the Sidewalk Ends* by Shel Silverstein. Copyright © 1974 by Shel Silverstein. By permission of Harper & Row, Publishers, Inc.

Illustrations: Ray Cruz, pp. 4-7; Jozef Sumichrast, pp. 12-25; Olivia Cole, pp. 28-29; Sims Taback, pp. 40-43; Joanne Scribner, pp. 46-51; Susan Swan, pp. 58-59; Philip Wende, pp. 60-77; Carveth, pp. 78-79; Lewis Friedland, pp. 88-89; Richard Brown, pp. 92-101; Kenneth Longtemps, pp. 102-103. **Photographs:** Norman Owen Tomalin/ Bruce Coleman, Inc., pp. 10-11; James Foote, pp. 82-87. **Cover Design:** AKM Associates

4

Contents

UPS AND DOWNS

Sometimes you help your family.
You help your friends work and play.
Your family and friends help you, too.
Many of the friends in "Ups and Downs"
help each other.
Other friends can't help each other.

As you read, look for friends
who can help each other.
Look for other friends
who don't help each other.

Things in the Pool

In this quiet pool
fish
glide
bugs
ride
snakes
slide
turtles
hide.

And in this quiet place
I
see
Me
looking up,
my
eyes
my
face.

—Lilian Moore

11

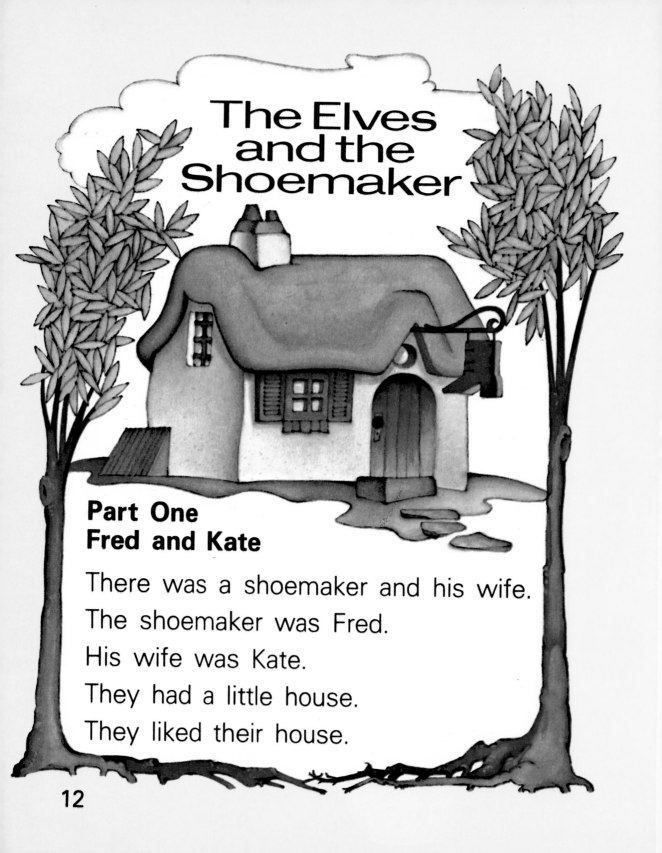

The Elves and the Shoemaker

Part One
Fred and Kate

There was a shoemaker and his wife.

The shoemaker was Fred.

His wife was Kate.

They had a little house.

They liked their house.

Fred liked to make shoes.
He liked to make shoes
for boys and girls.

Fred wanted leather to make shoes.
He had to have money for leather,
but Fred and Kate had no money.
So Fred and Kate were sad.

Fred did have a little leather.

He had leather for two shoes.

He cut it up.

Fred put the leather on his table.

He looked at the leather.

He had to have new leather!

Part Two
The Shoes

In the morning,
Fred went to make the shoes.
He looked at his table.
The shoes were made!
Who had made the shoes?
Fred and Kate didn't know.
But a man liked the shoes.
The man gave money to Fred.

Fred got new leather.
Now Fred and Kate were happy.
Fred cut up the leather.
He put it on his table.

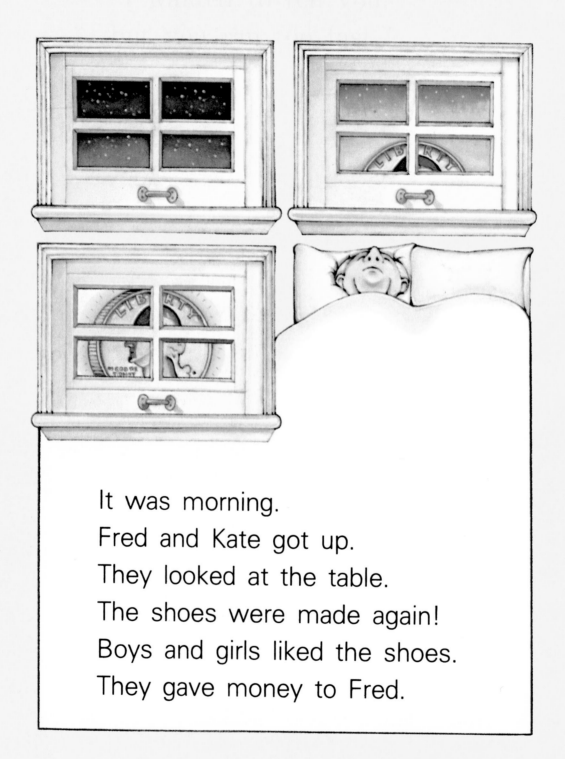

It was morning.
Fred and Kate got up.
They looked at the table.
The shoes were made again!
Boys and girls liked the shoes.
They gave money to Fred.

Each day, Fred got new leather.

He cut it up.

He put it on his table.

Each morning, the shoes were made.

Boys and girls liked the shoes.

They gave money to Fred.

Fred and Kate were happy.

Part Three
The Elves

One day, Fred said,
"I want to know
who makes the shoes.
Let's hide.
Then we can see who it is."
Kate said, "I like that.
We will hide."
So they went to hide.

Fred and Kate had to wait and wait.
Then they saw a funny thing.
Elves were in the house!
The elves went to the table.
They made the shoes.
Then the elves went out of the house.

In the morning, Kate said,
"I want to make a present
for the elves.
I will make new hats for the elves."
Fred said, "I like that.
I will make new shoes for the elves."
So Fred and Kate worked and worked.

Fred and Kate put the hats on the table.

They put the shoes there, too.

Then Fred and Kate went to hide.

Soon the elves were in the house.

They went to the table.

But there was no leather.

The elves saw the new hats.

They saw the new shoes.

The elves liked the new things.

They put on the hats and shoes.

The elves sang and laughed.

The elves were happy.

They ran out of the house.

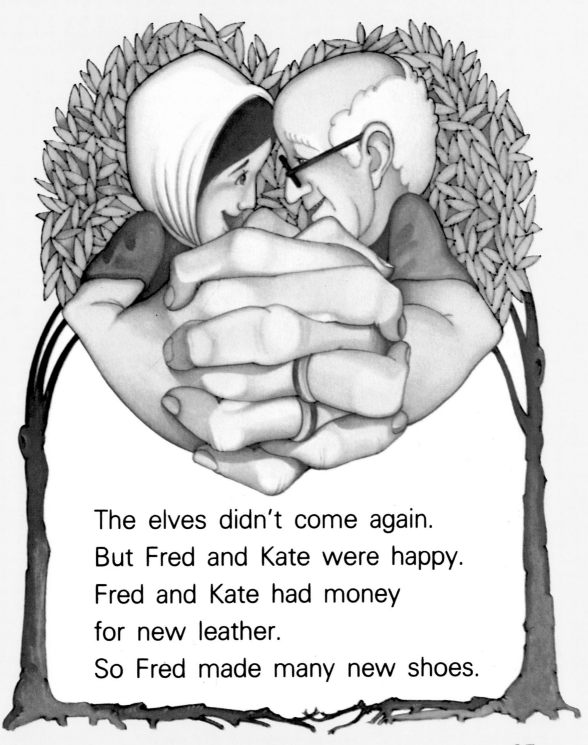

The elves didn't come again.
But Fred and Kate were happy.
Fred and Kate had money
for new leather.
So Fred made many new shoes.

The Magic e

What letter makes a word to name
each picture?
Write each word on your paper.

| a | i | o |

1. b_i_ke

2. l__ke

3. h__me

4. c__ke

5. b__ne

6. k__te

What letter makes a word that can
go in each sentence?
Write each sentence on your paper.

a	i	**1.** Mindy wanted to h__de.
o	a	**2.** Kate dr__ve to the park.
a	i	**3.** Jay played a g__me.
i	a	**4.** We can m__ke a bird happy.
o	i	**5.** I can tell the t__me.
o	a	**6.** Ann g__ve Grandma a picture.
a	o	**7.** We can walk h__me.

Put two words in a sentence.
Write each sentence on your paper.

a	o	**8.** We dr__ve to the pl__ce.
a	i	**9.** Hal g__ve his w__fe a present.
i	a	**10.** Kim will r__de to the l__ke.

I woke up one morning
Without any head,
So I jumped to the floor
And looked under the bed,
Then under my pillow,
The table,
The chair,
But look where I would,
My head wasn't there.

28

Not on the ceiling,
Not on the floor,
Not in the tree,
Not near the door.
Then at last I remembered—
Sure enough, just like that,
I found my old head!
It was under my hat.

—Arnold Spilka

A SURPRISE FOR GRANDMA

Lenore Israel

**Part One
Fun
With
Grandma**

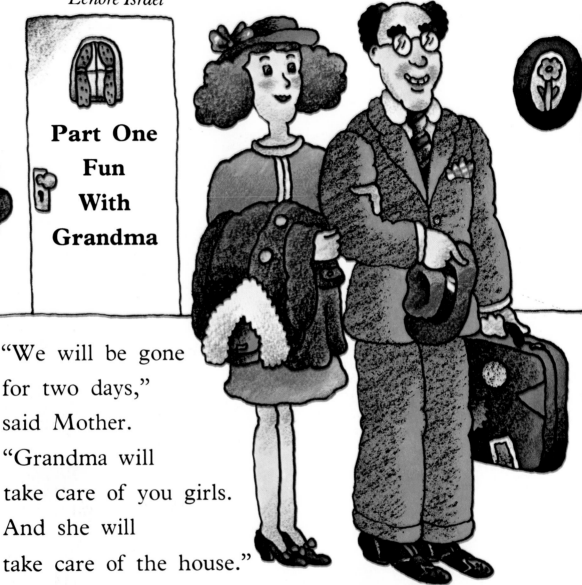

"We will be gone
for two days,"
said Mother.
"Grandma will
take care of you girls.
And she will
take care of the house."

"What can we do?"
asked Linda and Myra.

"You can be good girls," said Father.
"And you can have fun.
You can play and ride your bikes.
Grandma will take care of things."

The family said good-by.
Then Mother and Father were gone.

Grandma said to the girls,
"I like fun, too!
Linda, you take your red bike.
Myra, you take your green bike.
And I'll take the old bike
with no paint on it.
Let's ride to the park."

In the park Grandma said,
"I have a ball with me.
Let's play and have fun."

The two girls played ball
in the park with Grandma.

Then Grandma said,
"Let's ride home again.
Let's see who
can get there first."

Grandma got home first.
"It looks like rain," she said.

"Let's run to the house,"
said Linda.

"I like to run," said Myra.

"Me, too," said Grandma.
"Let's run!"

34

Part Two
The Girls Take Care of Things

In the morning Grandma said,
You girls go out and have fun.
I will sit in the house.
That will help my cold."

35

Linda and Myra were going out to play.
Then Linda said,
"Grandma wants to take care
of her cold.
Who will take care of things
in the house?"

Linda looked at Myra.
And Myra looked at Linda.

"We will," said the girls.

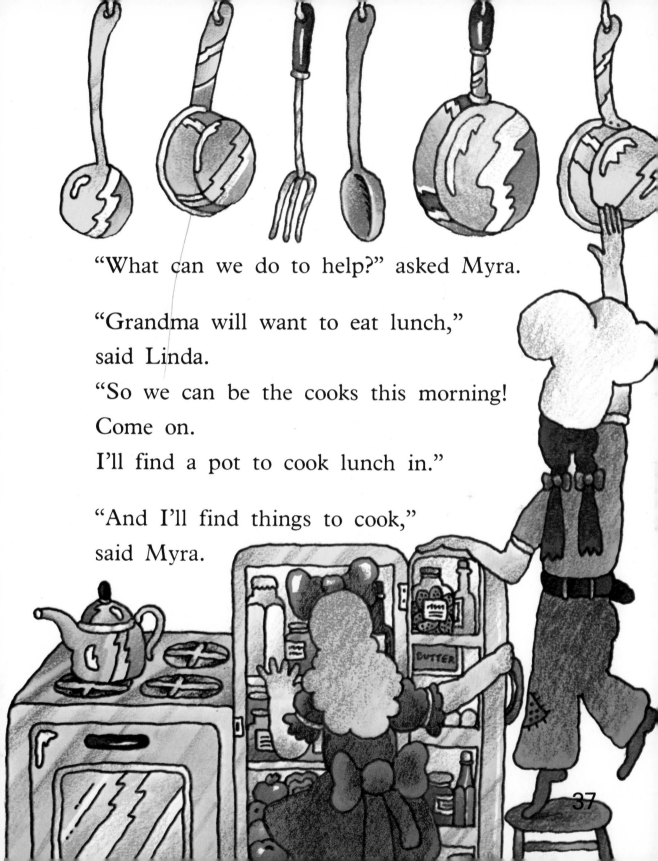

"What can we do to help?" asked Myra.

"Grandma will want to eat lunch,"
said Linda.
"So we can be the cooks this morning!
Come on.
I'll find a pot to cook lunch in."

"And I'll find things to cook,"
said Myra.

37

"Look!

I found a fish," said Myra.

"And here are two eggs."

"Fish and eggs go into the pot,"
said Linda.

"And here is a can of soup,"
said Myra.

"Soup into the pot!" said Linda.

"Fish and eggs and soup," said Linda.

"Lets' find one other thing to cook."

Myra looked and looked.
And then she said,
"I know!
Ice cream!
I love ice cream."

"Ice cream into the pot!" said Linda.

"Fish and eggs and soup for lunch,"
said Linda.

"And ice cream!" said Myra.
"What a surprise for Grandma!"

Grandma looked at her lunch,
and she laughed.
"This is a surprise!" she said.

Part Three
Mother and Father Come Home

Linda, Myra, and Grandma
were playing ball again.
A car
drove up.

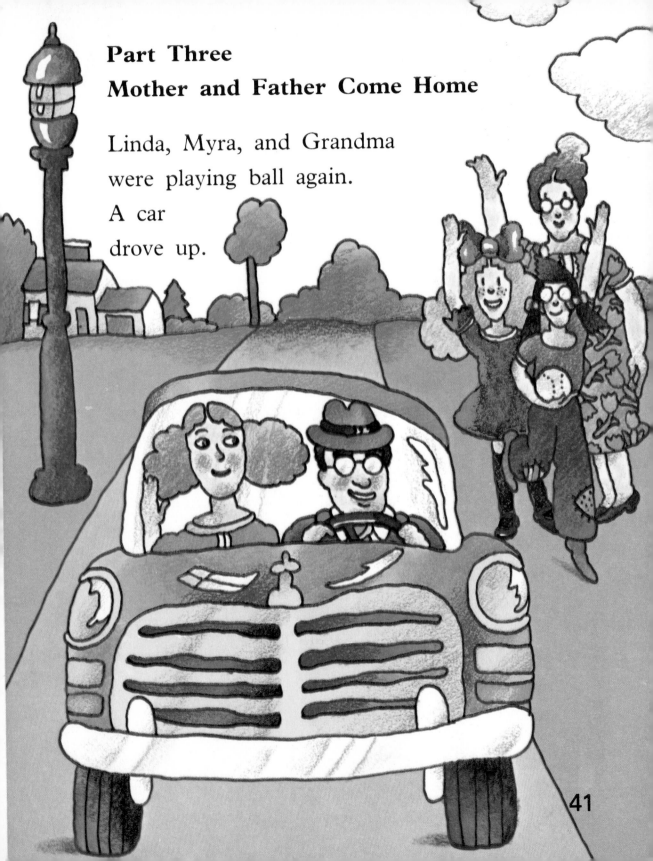

"Mother! Father!"
said Linda and Myra.

"I didn't think you liked to play ball,"
said Father to Grandma.

"But I do," said Grandma.
"And I love playing with the girls.
Linda and Myra were
a big help to me, too.
Tell what you did today, girls."

"Grandma wanted to take care
of her cold today," said Linda.
"So Myra and I gave her lunch."

"What did you cook for Grandma?"
asked Mother.

"We cooked something good,"
said Myra.
"When you have a cold,
we will cook something good for you."

"I think I'll like that," said Mother.

Grandma and the girls laughed.

If I Were a Sandwich

If I were a sandwich,
I'd sit on a plate
And think of my middle
Until someone ate
Me.
End of the sandwich.

—Karla Kuskin

John's Day

Norah Smaridge

Part One
John's Morning

It was a bad morning for John.
He looked at his frog,
and he looked at his things.
There were his crayons.
There were his paints.
And there was his boat.
But he was not happy,
and his things didn't help.

His mother looked at John.
"You don't look happy to me,"
she said.
"Why don't you play
with your crayons or your paints?"

"I don't want to.
That's why!" said John.

"Then why not take your frog
and go find Liza?" said his mother.

"No!" said John.
"Liza ran when she saw
my frog this morning.
She said she didn't like it."

"This **is** a bad morning for you,"
said his mother.
"Why don't you..."

But John didn't wait.
He ran out of the house
with his things.
And then—
he threw his boat
into the garbage can!

Liza was there,
and she saw what John did.

"Don't do that, John!
I love that red boat!" said Liza.

"I can do what I like
with my things," said John.
"**Look.**"

He threw his paints
into the garbage can.
He threw his crayons in, too.
Then he laughed.

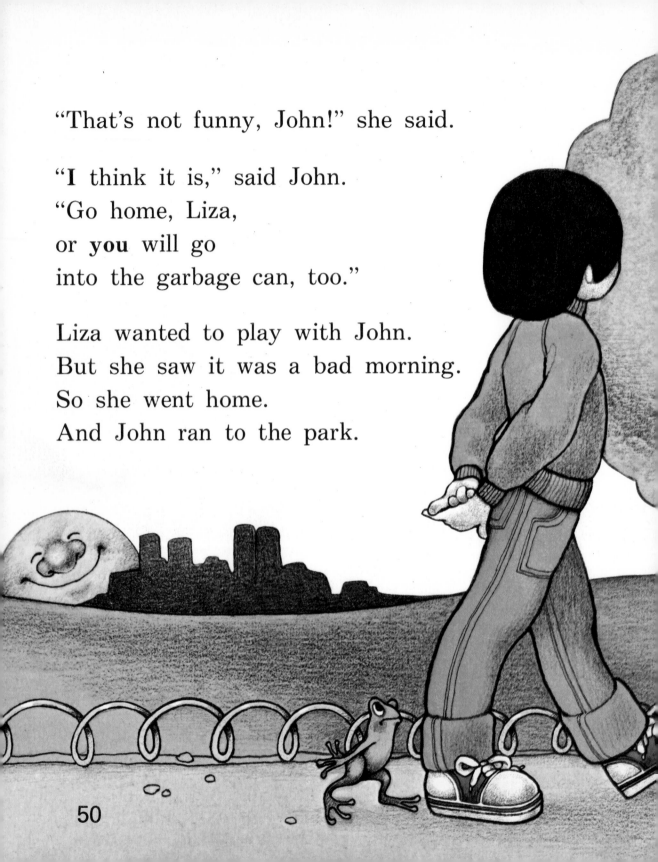

"That's not funny, John!" she said.

"I think it is," said John.
"Go home, Liza,
or **you** will go
into the garbage can, too."

Liza wanted to play with John.
But she saw it was a bad morning.
So she went home.
And John ran to the park.

50

Part Two
John's Afternoon

John ran into the park.
He thought of the morning.
He thought of the things
he threw out.
He thought of Liza.

He saw two little boys
with a big box.

"Let's break it," said one.
"Yes, let's break it," said the other.

John ran to the box.

"Don't break that box.
We can make a house
out of it," said John.
"Help me take it home."

52

John went home with the boys
and the box.

In the afternoon John looked
in the garbage can.
There were his paints
and his crayons.

"I'll paint the house," John said.
"And you can make windows."

"Let's make big windows,"
said the two little boys.

Mother saw the house.

"I love the windows!" she said.
"I'll make you a door.
Then you can go in."

When there was a door,
the boys went into the house.
And so did John's frog.

Then a girl looked in
the door.
It was Liza.

"You can't come in," said John.
"My frog is in here with me.
And you don't like it."

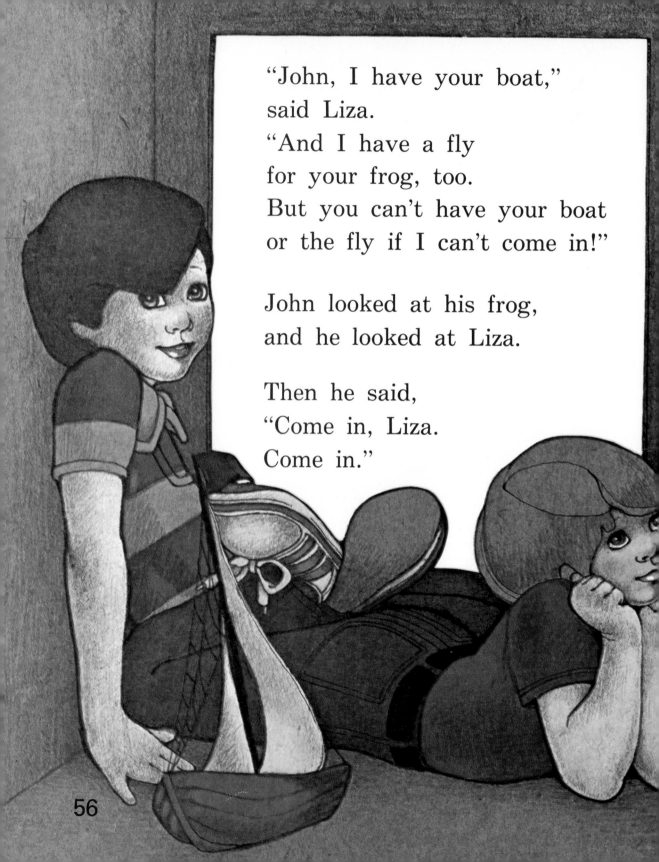

"John, I have your boat,"
said Liza.
"And I have a fly
for your frog, too.
But you can't have your boat
or the fly if I can't come in!"

John looked at his frog,
and he looked at Liza.

Then he said,
"Come in, Liza.
Come in."

It was a bad morning.
But it was a good afternoon.

I wonder how it feels to fly
high in the sky . . .
    like a bird.

I wonder how it feels to sit
on a nest . . .
    like a bird.

I wonder how it feels to catch
a worm in the morning . . .
    like a bird.

I feel funny . . .
maybe it is wondering
    how it feels to be like a child.

—Yakima

59

Silly Sam

Leonore Klein

Part One
A Fish for Alice

Silly Sam was going to a party.

It was a party for Alice.

He put on his shoes.

He put on his hat.

He put on his coat.

And he went to the party.

Si[...] ent by a man
[...]

"I am going to a party for Alice,"
said Silly Sam.
"Do you know what present
I can give her?
She has books and hats
and balls and crayons.
She has all kinds of things
to play with.
What present can I give her?"

"Does she have a fish
that can jump up and down?"
asked the man.

"No," said Silly Sam.

"I will give you a fish
that can jump up and down,"
said the man.
"Stop by a lake and put in the fish.
He will jump up and down.
But you have to give me your shoes."

Silly Sam wanted a present
for Alice.
So he gave the man his shoes.

Silly Sam went by a lake.

"I will stop and put in the fish,"
said Silly Sam.
"I want to see it jump
up and down."

Silly Sam put in the fish.

"Jump!" he said.

But the fish did not jump.
Sam looked, and the fish was gone.
"Stop!" called Silly Sam.
But the fish did not stop.

"What will I do?"
said Silly Sam.
"Alice has all kinds of things
to play with.
I have no present for her.
And I have no shoes."

Part Two
The Fly That Was Not There

Silly Sam went on his way.
He saw a boy with a box.

"I will stop and ask this boy
if he can help me," said Silly Sam.

"I am on my way to a party
for Alice," said Silly Sam.
"Do you know what
present I can give her?
She has books and hats
and balls and crayons.
She has all kinds
of things to play with."

"Does she have a fly
that no one can see?"
asked the boy.

"No," said Silly Sam.

"I will give you a fly
that no one can see," said the boy.
"But you have to give me your hat."

Silly Sam wanted a present
for Alice.
So he gave the boy his hat.

Silly Sam wanted to see the fly.
So he looked in the box.
But he didn't see a fly.
He looked and looked.
But there was no fly in the box.

"What will I do?" said Silly Sam.
"I have no present for Alice.
I have no shoes, and I have no hat."

Silly Sam went on his way.

Part Three
Good-by, Bird

Silly Sam saw a little girl
with a gold cage.
There was a gold bird in the cage.

"I am on my way to a party
for Alice," said Silly Sam.
"Do you know what present
I can give her?
She has books and hats
and balls and crayons.
She has all kinds of things
to play with."

"Does she have a bird
that can fly very high?"
asked the little girl.

"No," said Silly Sam.

"I will give you a bird
that can fly very high.
But you have to give me your coat."

Silly Sam wanted a present
for Alice.
So he gave the girl his coat.

Silly Sam wanted to see
the bird fly very high.
So he looked in the gold cage.
And the bird flew out.
It flew up high.
It flew up very high.
Then it flew away.

"What will I do?" said Silly Sam.
"I have no present for Alice.
The fish did not jump up and down.
There was no fly in the box.
The bird flew away.
And I gave away my shoes, my hat,
and my coat."

Part Four
At the Party

Silly Sam was very sad.
He looked back at the cage.
Then he looked back
at the cage again.
And he saw a little gold egg.

"I will go to the party," said Silly Sam.
"And I will give Alice this egg.
I have no other present for her."

The girls and the boys at the party
laughed at Silly Sam.
There he was
without shoes,
without a hat,
and without a coat on his back.
And the boys and girls laughed
at his little present, too.

But Alice looked at the egg.
And, as she looked, it cracked.
And then it cracked a little more.
And then it cracked a little more.

There, in the egg,
was a little gold bird.
It was a little gold bird
for Alice.

"A gold bird!" said Alice.
"I love my present, Sam.
I do!"

Silly Sam had no shoes.
He had no hat.
And he had no coat.
But he didn't care.
He had a happy friend.

78

Things That Go Together

Thunder and lightning go together.
So do hands and mittens,

Beans and rice, fire and ice,
Mother cats and kittens.

News and weather go together.
So do reading and writing,
Fish and bones!
Ice cream and cones!
Also, loving and fighting.

Betty Miles and Joan Blos

What Is the Question?

Sentences that ask something are
called question sentences.
Write the question sentences on
your paper.

1. Is it John's surprise party?

1. Is it John's surprise party?

2. Alice had fun at the party.

3. Did Linda come to the party?

4. Kate can ride her bike to
the party.

5. Did John want all his friends at
the party?

6. Who will come to the party?

7. We ate ice cream at the party.

8. Do you like ice cream?

9. Did Sam have a present?

A sentence that asks something must have a question mark at the end. Write the sentences that must have question marks. Then put the question mark in each sentence.

1. Do you love your grandma

   1. Do you love your grandma?

2. I love my grandma
3. Where is my grandma
4. Grandma is my friend
5. Did Myra cook an egg
6. Myra cooks an egg each day
7. Who cooked an egg
8. Ben eats ice cream each day
9. Who eats ice cream each day
10. Does Ben eat ice cream
11. Sam had a happy friend

Rosa and Her Shadow

Judith Adams

When Rosa goes out to play,

she is not alone.

Her shadow is there.

She can't go out without it.

Or can she?

She puts on her hat and goes out.

Rosa is quiet, very quiet.

She thinks she is alone.

Then she slowly looks back.

And what does she see?

Her shadow!

She was so quiet, too.

Rosa takes her time as she walks.
And her shadow takes its time, too.
Then she sees her friends
and she runs.
And her shadow runs
to be there with her.

When Rosa goes home to eat,
she is not alone.
Her shadow is there all the time.

What if Rosa wants to be alone?
She can't put her shadow in a box.
And she can't give it away.
How **do** you say good-by to a shadow?

DO YOU KNOW?

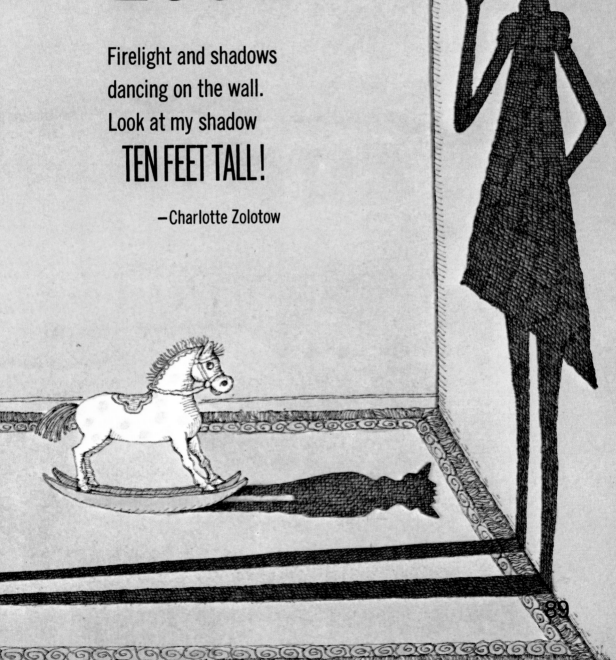

Look

Firelight and shadows
dancing on the wall.
Look at my shadow
TEN FEET TALL!

—Charlotte Zolotow

Think!

Look at the word in the box.

Think what the word in the box means.

Write each sentence on your paper.

A │ kitten │ likes to play.

A │ kitten │ is little and funny.

1. A │ kitten │ is _____.

   a little cat

   a house

1. A kitten is a little cat.

A │ dictionary │ is something you can read.

A │ dictionary │ tells about words.

2. A │ dictionary │ is _____.

   a lizard

   a book

90

A pond has frogs in it.

You can fish in a pond .

3. A pond is ———.

    a small lake

    a crayon

A canary can fly.

A canary can be in a cage.

4. A canary is ———.

    a little bird

    a green bike

A cafeteria is a place to eat.

People have lunch in a cafeteria .

5. A cafeteria is ———.

    a pony

    a lunchroom

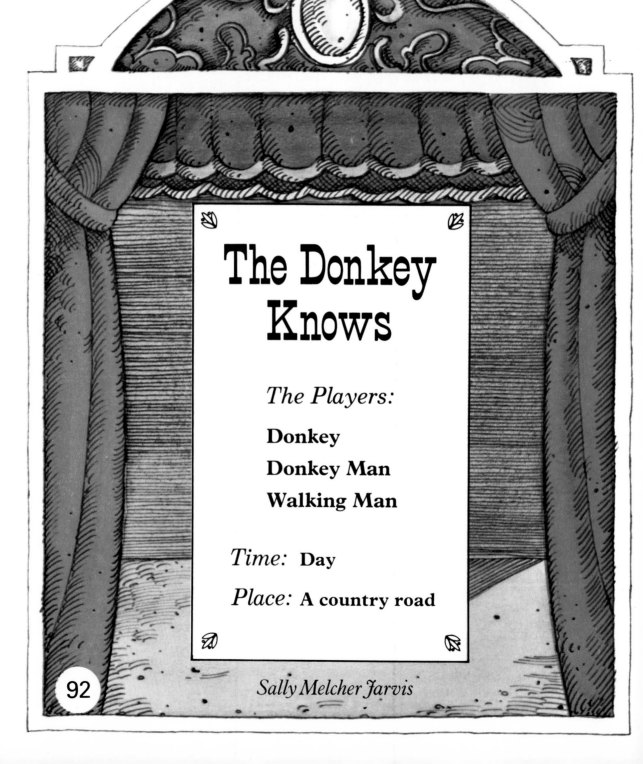

The Donkey Knows

The Players:

Donkey

Donkey Man

Walking Man

Time: **Day**

Place: **A country road**

Sally Melcher Jarvis

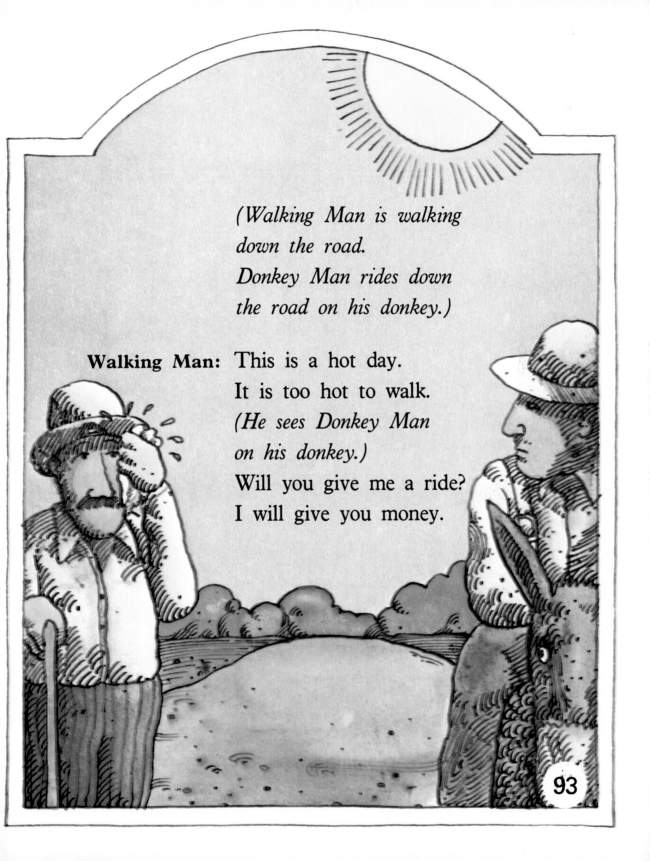

*(Walking Man is walking
down the road.
Donkey Man rides down
the road on his donkey.)*

Walking Man: This is a hot day.
It is too hot to walk.
*(He sees Donkey Man
on his donkey.)*
Will you give me a ride?
I will give you money.

Donkey Man: Yes!

Give me your money.

Walking Man: Here you are.

(He gives Donkey Man money, and he jumps on Donkey.)

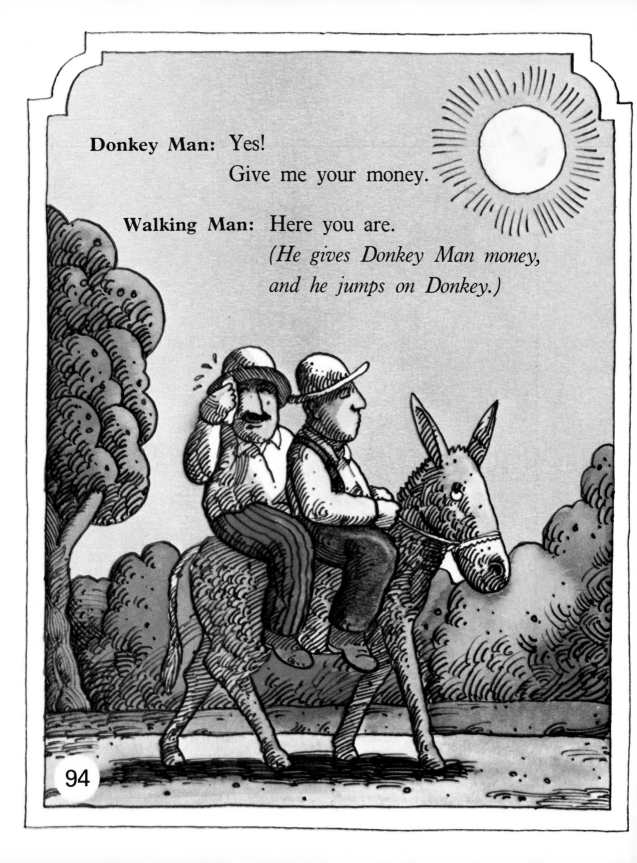

Donkey Man: How hot it is!
I think I will stop for water.

Donkey: *(to himself)*
Will they think of me?
*(Walking Man and Donkey Man
stop for water.
They don't give water to Donkey.)*

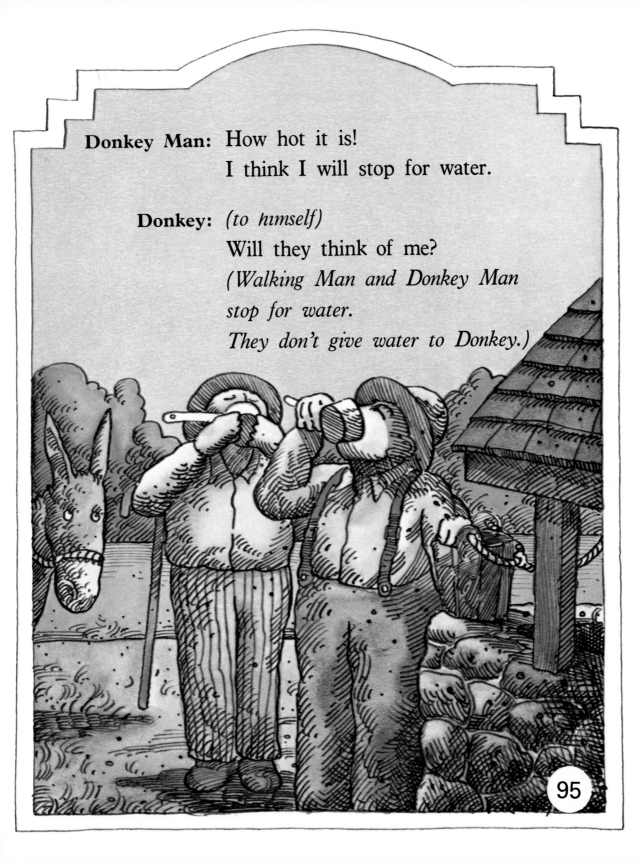

Donkey: *(to himself)* I am hot,
but they didn't give me water.

Walking Man: I think I will sit down.

Donkey: *(to himself)*
Can't I sit down, too?

Walking Man: It is so hot!
I think I will sit
in the shadow of the donkey!

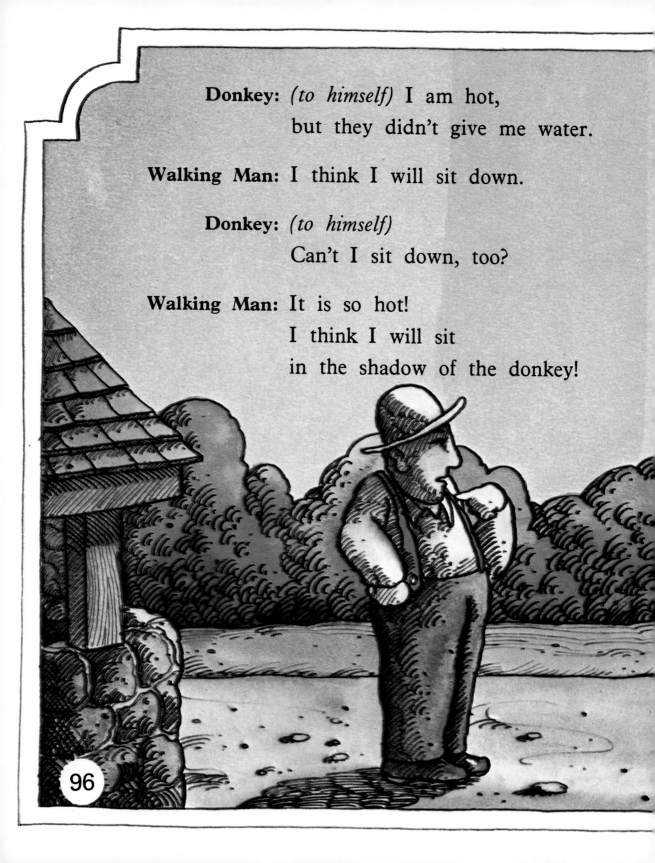

Donkey Man: No, you don't!
There is a place for one man here.
It is **my** donkey.
I think I will sit in his shadow.

Walking Man: I gave you money.
I will sit there!
*(He sits down in the shadow
of Donkey.)*

Donkey Man: You gave me money
to ride my donkey.
You didn't give me money
to sit in his shadow.
I will sit there!
*(He pushes Walking Man
out of the shadow.)*

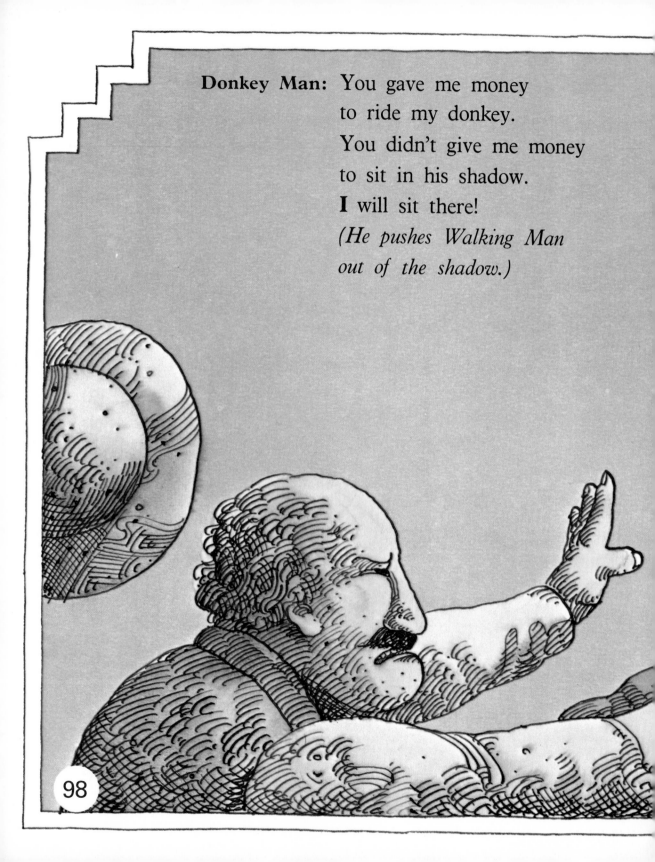

Walking Man: Don't do that!
(*He pushes Donkey Man,
and he pushes Donkey.*)

Donkey: (*to himself*)
I think I will run away!
(*He runs away.*)

Donkey Man: Come back! Come back!

Walking Man: He is gone!

Donkey Man: It is so hot.
And we have to walk.
There is no shadow for you
or for me.

Walking Man: Why do you think the donkey
ran away?

Donkey Man: I don't know.

Walking Man: And **I** don't know.

Donkey: *(He is down the road.*
He looks back.)
I know why!

Tree House

A tree house, a free house,
A secret you and me house,
A high up in the leafy branches
Cozy as can be house.

A street house, a neat house,
Be sure and wipe your feet house
Is not my kind of house at all —
Let's go live in a tree house.

—Shel Silverstein

UPS AND DOWNS

In "Ups and Downs," you read about
friends who helped each other.
They helped each other do things
and find things.
You read about friends who didn't
help each other, too.

Thinking About "Ups and Downs"

1. How did the elves
   help Fred and Kate?
2. What did the girls do
   to help their Grandma?
3. Why do you think Donkey Man
   and Walking Man didn't help Donkey?
4. What things do you do to help
   your family and friends?

Word List

12. elves   15. *cut*
    shoemaker   put
    Fred   table
    wife   16. morning
13. shoes   *made*
14. leather   17. *got*
    money   26. *name*
                   27. *Grandma*

To the Teacher: The words listed beside the page numbers above are introduced in "Ups and Downs," Level 8 of SERIES r. The children should be able to use previously taught skills to identify the italicized words independently.

30. *take*

    care

    asked

    Linda

    Myra

31. good

    fun

    bikes

    good-by

32. *bike*

33. ball

    get

35. cold

37. eat

    lunch

    cooks

    pot

    cook

38. eggs

    soup

39. ice

    cream

    love

41. playing

42. think

    today

43. *cooked*

    something

    when

46. John's

    bad

    John

    frog

    crayons

    boat

47. Liza

48. threw

    garbage

51. afternoon

    thought

52. break

53. windows

54. door

60. silly

    Sam

    Alice

    coat

61.	by	65.	*called*
	am	66.	way
	give	70.	gold
	has		cage
	books	71.	very
	balls	72.	flew
	all		away
	kinds	74.	*back*
62.	stop		*egg*
	must	75.	*without*

76. cracked

more

80. question

81. *asks*

mark

end

marks

82. Rosa

shadow

goes

alone

puts

quiet

thinks

84. *takes*

its

86. how

90. means
91. *book*
92. donkey
    knows
    players
    walking
    road
93. *hot*
94. *gives*

95. water
    himself
98. pushes
104. *helped*